92 Powerful Juice and Meal Recipes to Recover From Hangovers:

Get Back on Track Quickly Using These Effective Ingredients

By

Joe Correa CSN

COPYRIGHT

© 2019 Live Stronger Faster Inc.

All rights reserved

Reproduction or translation of any part of this work beyond that permitted by section 107 or 108 of the 1976 United States Copyright Act without the permission of the copyright owner is unlawful.

This publication is designed to provide accurate and authoritative information in regard to the subject matter covered. It is sold with the understanding that neither the author nor the publisher is engaged in rendering medical advice. If medical advice or assistance is needed, consult with a doctor. This book is considered a guide and should not be used in any way detrimental to your health. Consult with a physician before starting this nutritional plan to make sure it's right for you.

ACKNOWLEDGEMENTS

This book is dedicated to my friends and family that have had mild or serious illnesses so that you may find a solution and make the necessary changes in your life.

92 Powerful Juice and Meal Recipes to Recover From Hangovers:

Get Back on Track Quickly Using These Effective Ingredients

By

Joe Correa CSN

92 Powerful Juice and Meal Recipes to Recover From Hangovers

CONTENTS

Copyright

Acknowledgements

About The Author

Introduction

Commitment

92 Powerful Juice and Meal Recipes to Recover From Hangovers: Get Back on Track Quickly Using These Effective Ingredients

Additional Titles from This Author

ABOUT THE AUTHOR

After years of Research, I honestly believe in the positive effects that proper nutrition can have over the body and mind. My knowledge and experience has helped me live healthier throughout the years and which I have shared with family and friends. The more you know about eating and drinking healthier, the sooner you will want to change your life and eating habits.

Nutrition is a key part in the process of being healthy and living longer so get started today. The first step is the most important and the most significant.

INTRODUCTION

92 Powerful Juice and Meal Recipes to Recover From Hangovers: Get Back on Track Quickly Using These Effective Ingredients

By Joe Correa CSN

As we all know, most symptoms are completely harmless and usually go away on their own the next day. If some of the symptoms don't go away on their own or you feel them more intensively than usual, it's a good idea to visit your doctor. In other cases, all you have to do is stay in bed and clean your body through healthy food.

Preventing a hangover is not difficult, drinking responsibly is the only way of preventing this unpleasant and even painful condition. However, on some occasions this may be easier said than done. This is why you should consider some powerful healing methods that will clean your body from within and help you reduce most hangover symptoms much faster than before.

The number one thing you can do for yourself is to hydrate your body with a good juice based on healthy ingredients your body needs. The right combination of detoxifying fruits and vegetables will reduce the damage alcohol has made in your body and help your organism heal.

This book is all about that! It's the best collection of carefully chosen recipes that will reduce hangover symptoms and help you recover in no time at all. Find the best recipes and enjoy!

COMMITMENT

In order to improve my condition, I *(your name)*, commit to eating more of these foods on a daily basis and to exercise at least 30 minutes daily:

- Berries (especially blueberries), peaches, cherries, apples, apricots, oranges, lemon juice, grapefruit, tangerines, mandarins, pears, etc.
- Broccoli, spinach, collard greens, sweet potatoes, avocado, artichoke, baby corn, carrots, celery, cauliflower, onions, etc.
- Whole grains, steel-cut oats, oatmeal, quinoa, barley, etc.
- Black beans, red bean beans, garbanzo beans, lentils, etc.
- Nuts and seeds including: walnuts, cashews, flaxseeds, sesame seeds, etc.
- Fish
- 8 – 10 glasses of water

Sign here

X_____

92 POWERFUL JUICE AND MEAL RECIPES TO RECOVER FROM HANGOVERS: GET BACK ON TRACK QUICKLY USING THESE EFFECTIVE INGREDIENTS

1. Orange Marmite Juice

Ingredients:

1 large orange, peeled

2 oz coconut water

1 cup fresh cranberries

1 cup fresh strawberries

1 tsp marmite

Preparation:

Peel the orange and divide into wedges. Set aside.

Combine cranberries and strawberries in a colander and rinse under cold running water. Drain and set aside.

Combine orange, cranberries, and strawberries in a juicer and process until juiced.

Transfer to serving glasses and stir in the coconut water

and marmite. Optionally, add some cinnamon for some extra flavour.

Add some ice and serve immediately.

Nutrition information per serving: Kcal: 147, Protein: 3.1g, Carbs: 52.7g, Fats: 0.9g

2.　Watermelon Honey Juice

Ingredients:

1 cup watermelon, seeded

1 tbsp liquid honey

1 cup fresh blueberries

1 cup fresh raspberries

1 cup fresh cranberries

1 large lemon, peeled

Preparation:

Cut the watermelon lengthwise. For one cup, you will need about 1 large wedge. Peel and cut into chunks. Remove the seeds and set aside. Reserve the rest of the melon for some other juices.

Combine blueberries, raspberries, and cranberries in a colander and rinse under cold running water. Drain and set aside.

Peel the lemon and cut lengthwise in half. Set aside.

Now, process watermelon, blueberries, raspberries, cranberries, and lemon in a juicer.

Transfer to serving glasses and stir in the liquid honey.

Add some ice cubes before serving.

Enjoy!

Nutrition information per serving: Kcal: 230, Protein: 4.1g, Carbs: 53.1g, Fats: 1.7g

3. Grapefruit Lime Juice

Ingredients:

1 whole grapefruit, peeled

1 whole lime, peeled

1 cup asparagus, trimmed and chopped

1 whole leek, chopped

1 oz water

Preparation:

Peel the grapefruit and divide into wedges. Cut each wedge in half and set aside.

Peel the lime and cut lengthwise in half. Set aside.

Wash the asparagus and trim off the woody ends. Chop into small pieces and set aside.

Wash the leek and cut into bite-sized pieces. Set aside.

Now, combine grapefruit, lime, asparagus, and leek in a juicer and process until well juiced. Transfer to a serving glass and stir in the water.

Refrigerate for 5 minutes before serving.

Enjoy!

Nutritional information per serving: Kcal: 161, Protein: 6.3g, Carbs: 47.7g, Fats: 0.8g

4. Watermelon Lemon Juice

Ingredients:

1 cup watermelon, chopped

1 whole lemon, peeled

1 cup cranberries

1 cup fresh mint, chopped

1 tbsp liquid honey

Preparation:

Cut the watermelon lengthwise. For one cup, you will need a large slice. Peel and cut into chunks. Remove the seeds and set aside. Reserve the rest for some other juices.

Peel the lemon and cut lengthwise in half. Set aside.

Wash the cranberries using a colander. Fill the measuring cup and reserve the rest in the refrigerator.

Wash the mint thoroughly under cold running water and roughly chop it. Set aside.

Now, combine watermelon, lemon, cranberries, and mint in a juicer and process until juiced. Transfer to a serving glass and stir in the honey.

Add few ice cubes and serve immediately.

Enjoy!

Nutritional information per serving: Kcal: 93, Protein: 2.9g, Carbs: 32.8g, Fats: 0.7g

5. Ginger Orange Juice

Ingredients:

1 small ginger knob, peeled and chopped

1 medium-sized orange, peeled

2 cups blueberries

1 cup black grapes

Preparation:

Peel the ginger and cut into small pieces. Set aside.

Peel the orange and divide into wedges. Cut each wedge in half and set aside.

Place the blueberries in a colander. Wash thoroughly under cold running water and drain. Fill the measuring cups and reserve the rest in the freezer.

Rinse the grapes and fill the measuring cup. Set aside.

Now, combine ginger, orange, blueberries, and grapes in a juicer and process until juiced. Transfer to a serving glass and add few ice cubes before serving.

Nutritional information per serving: Kcal: 254, Protein: 4.1g, Carbs: 75.2g, Fats: 1.5g

6. Apple Carrot Juice

Ingredients:

1 small Granny Smith's apple, cored

1 medium-sized carrot, sliced

1 cup pumpkin, cubed

1 cup cucumber, sliced

¼ tsp cinnamon, ground

¼ tsp ginger, ground

Preparation:

Wash the apple and cut lengthwise in half. Remove the core and cut into small pieces. Set aside.

Wash and peel the carrot. Cut into thin slices and set aside.

Cut the pumpkin in half and scoop out the seeds. Wash it and cut one large wedge. Peel it and cut into small cubes. Fill the measuring cup and reserve the rest in the refrigerator.

Wash the cucumber and cut into thin slices. Fill the measuring cup and reserve the rest for later.

Now, combine apple, carrot, pumpkin, and cucumber in a juicer and process until juiced. Transfer to a serving glass and stir in the cinnamon and ginger.

Refrigerate for 5 minutes before serving.

Nutritional information per serving: Kcal: 121, Protein: 2.7g, Carbs: 34.8g, Fats: 0.6g

7. Pear Plum Juice

Ingredients:

1 medium-sized pear, chopped

1 whole plum, pitted

1 medium-sized orange, peeled

1 whole lemon, peeled

1 oz water

Preparation:

Wash the pear and cut in half. Remove the core and chop into small pieces. Set aside.

Wash the plum and cut in half. Remove the pit and cut in small pieces.

Peel the orange and divide into wedges. Cut each wedge in half and set aside.

Peel the lemon and cut into quarters. Set aside.

Now, combine pear, plum, orange, and lemon in a juicer and process until juiced. Transfer to a serving glass and stir in the water.

You can add a pinch of minced mint for some extra smooth flavor, but it's optional.

Add some crushed ice and serve immediately.

Nutritional information per serving: Kcal: 166, Protein: 2.9g, Carbs: 55.4g, Fats: 0.8g

8. Avocado Ginger Juice

Ingredients:

1 cup avocado, cubed

1 medium-sized apple, cored

2 cups blackberries

¼ tsp ginger, ground

Preparation:

Peel the avocado and cut lengthwise in half. Remove the pit and cut into small cubes. Fill the measuring cup and reserve the rest in the refrigerator.

Wash the apple and cut in half. Remove the core and cut into bite-sized pieces. Set aside.

Place the blackberries in a colander and wash thoroughly under cold running water. Slightly drain and set aside.

Now, combine avocado, apple, and blackberries in a juicer and process until juiced. Transfer to a serving glass and stir in the ginger.

Add some ice and serve immediately.

Nutritional information per serving: Kcal: 342, Protein: 7.7g, Carbs: 63.2g, Fats: 23.7g

9. Lemon Lime Juice

Ingredients:

1 whole lemon, peeled

1 whole lime, peeled

1 cup mango, chunked

1 small green apple, cored

1 tbsp coconut water

1 oz water

¼ tsp cinnamon, ground

Preparation:

Peel the lemon and lime. Cut each fruit in half and set aside.

Peel the mango and cut into small chunks. Fill the measuring cup and reserve the rest for later.

Wash the apple and cut in half. Remove the core and cut into bite-sized pieces. Set aside.

Now, combine lemon, lime, mango, and apple in a juicer and process until juiced. Transfer to a serving glass and stir in the coconut water, water, and cinnamon.

Add some crushed ice and serve immediately.

Nutritional information per serving: Kcal: 178, Protein: 2.8g, Carbs: 53.4g, Fats: 1.1g

10. Kiwi Cantaloupe Juice

Ingredients:

2 whole kiwis, peeled

1 cup cantaloupe, diced

1 whole lemon, peeled

1 cup blueberries

1 tbsp coconut water

Preparation:

Peel the kiwis and lemon. Cut lengthwise in half and set aside.

Cut the cantaloupe in half. Scoop out the seeds and cut one large wedge. Peel it and cut into small pieces. Fill the measuring cup and reserve the rest of the cantaloupe in a refrigerator.

Place the blueberries in a colander. Wash thoroughly and drain. Set aside.

Now, combine kiwis, cantaloupe, lemon and blueberries in a juicer and process until juiced. Transfer to a serving glass and stir in the coconut water.

Refrigerate for 15 minutes before serving.

Nutritional information per serving: Kcal: 196, Protein: 4.6g, Carbs: 59.8g, Fats: 1.6g

11. Carrot Orange Juice

Ingredients:

1 cup of beet greens, torn

1 large carrot, sliced

1 medium-sized orange, peeled

1 cup of cantaloupe, chopped

¼ tsp of ginger, ground

Preparation:

Wash the carrot and cut into thin slices. Set aside.

Peel the orange and divide into wedges. Cut each wedge in half and set aside.

Wash the beet greens thoroughly under cold running water. Drain and torn with hands. Set aside.

Cut the cantaloupe in half. Scoop out the seeds and cut one large wedge. Peel it and cut into small pieces. Fill the measuring cup and reserve the rest of the cantaloupe in a refrigerator.

Now, combine carrot, orange, beet greens, and cantaloupe in a juicer and process until juiced. Transfer to a serving glass and stir in the ginger.

Serve immediately.

Nutritional information per serving: Kcal: 99, Protein: 3.5g, Carbs: 30.5g, Fats: 0.6g

12. Broccoli Brussels Sprout Juice

Ingredients:

1 cup broccoli, chopped

1 cup Brussels sprouts, halved

1 cup fennel, chopped

1 cup watercress, torn

1 cup cucumber, sliced

Preparation:

Wash the broccoli and cut into small pieces. Fill the measuring cup and reserve the rest in the refrigerator. Set aside.

Wash the Brussels sprouts and trim off the outer layers. Cut in half and set aside.

Wash the fennel and trim off the outer leaves. Using a sharp paring knife, cut into small pieces and fill the measuring cup. Reserve the rest for later.

Wash the watercress thoroughly under cold running water. Slightly drain and torn with hands. Set aside.

Wash the cucumber and cut into thin slices. Fill the measuring cup and reserve the rest for later.

Now, combine broccoli, Brussels sprouts, fennel, watercress, and cucumber in a juicer and process until juiced. Transfer to a serving glass and refrigerate for 10 minutes before serving.

Enjoy!

Nutritional information per serving: Kcal: 72, Protein: 7.7g, Carbs: 22.6g, Fats: 0.8g

13. Spinach Beans Juice

Ingredients:

1 cup of fresh spinach, chopped

1 cup of green beans, chopped

1 medium-sized artichoke, chopped

1 small green bell pepper, sliced

1 small ginger knob, peeled and sliced

Preparation:

Using a colander, rinse the spinach thoroughly under cold running water. Chop into small pieces and set aside.

Place the beans in a deep pot. Add one cup of water and bring it to a boil. Cook for 5 minutes and remove from the heat. Set aside to cool completely.

Trim off the outer leaves of the artichoke using a sharp paring knife. Wash it and cut into bite-sized pieces. Set aside.

Wash the bell pepper and cut in half. Remove the seeds and stem. Cut into small rings and set aside.

Peel the ginger knob and chop it into small pieces. Set aside.

Now, combine spinach, green beans, artichoke, bell pepper, and ginger in a juicer and process until juiced. Transfer to a serving glass and refrigerate for 15 minutes before serving.

Nutritional information per serving: Kcal: 95, Protein: 11.9g, Carbs: 29.4g, Fats: 1.3g

14. Pear Coconut Juice

Ingredients:

1 medium-sized pear, chopped

1 cup crookneck squash, sliced

1 cup cucumber, sliced

1 whole lime, peeled

1 oz coconut water

Preparation:

Wash the pear and cut in half. Remove the core and chop into small pieces. Set aside.

Peel the crookneck squash and scrape out the seeds with a spoon. Cut into small cubes and fill the measuring cup. Reserve the rest of the squash for some other recipe. Wrap in a plastic foil and refrigerate.

Wash the cucumber and cut into thin slices. Fill the measuring cup and reserve the rest in the refrigerator. Set aside.

Peel the lime and cut lengthwise in half. Set aside.

Now, combine pear, squash, cucumber, and lime in a juicer. Process until juiced. Transfer to a serving glass and stir in the coconut water.

Add some ice and serve immediately.

Nutritional information per serving: Kcal: 120, Protein: 2.4g, Carbs: 37.6g, Fats: 0.7g

15. Cauliflower Spinach Juice

Ingredients:

1 cup fresh spinach, torn

1 cup pomegranate seeds

½ cup cauliflower, chopped

1 oz water

¼ tsp ginger, ground

Preparation:

Rinse the spinach thoroughly under running water. Torn with hands and set aside.

Cut the top of the pomegranate fruit using a sharp paring knife. Slice down to each of the white membranes inside of the fruit. Pop the seeds into a measuring cup and set aside.

Wash the cauliflower flowerets and chop into small pieces. Fill the measuring cup and reserve the rest for later.

Now, combine spinach, pomegranate, and cauliflower in a juicer and process until juiced. Transfer to a serving glass and stir in the water and ginger.

Add some ice and serve immediately.

Nutritional information per serving: Kcal: 162, Protein: 3.1g, Carbs: 47,6g, Fats: 1.6g

16. Zucchini Broccoli Juice

Ingredients:

1 medium-sized zucchini, sliced

2 cups fresh broccoli

1 cup mustard greens, torn

1 large grapefruit, peeled

1 cup Iceberg lettuce, torn

2 oz water

Preparation:

Peel the zucchini and cut in half. Scrape out the seeds and cut into small chunks. Set aside.

Rinse the broccoli and chop into small pieces. Set aside.

Combine mustard greens and lettuce in a colander. Wash under cold running water and torn with hands. Set aside.

Peel the grapefruit and divide into wedges. Set aside.

Now, process zucchini, broccoli, mustard greens, grapefruit, and lettuce in a juicer. Transfer to serving glasses and add some ice.

Serve immediately.

Nutrition information per serving: Kcal: 166, Protein: 11.6g, Carbs: 48.6g, Fats: 2.1g

17. Cinnamon Berry Juice

Ingredients:

1 cup strawberries, chopped

1 cup raspberries

1 cup cranberries

1 cup blackberries

1 cup blueberries

3 oz coconut water

¼ tsp cinnamon, ground

Preparation:

Combine strawberries, raspberries, cranberries blackberries, and blueberries in a colander. Rinse well under cold running water. Chop the strawberries and set aside.

Now, combine all in a juicer and process until juiced.

Transfer to serving glasses and stir in the coconut water and cinnamon.

Add some ice before serving.

Enjoy!

Nutrition information per serving: Kcal: 211, Protein: 5.9g, Carbs: 75.5g, Fats: 2.5g

18. Sweet Coconut Juice

Ingredients:

¼ cup pure coconut water, unsweetened

1 tbsp pure coconut sugar

1 large guava, chopped

1 ginger root slice, peeled

4 cups Swiss chard, torn

4 cups fresh kale, torn

A bunch of spinach, torn

Preparation:

Peel the guava and cut into chunks. Set aside.

Peel the ginger slice and set aside.

Combine Swiss chard, kale, and spinach in a colander and rinse thoroughly under cold running water. Drain and torn with hands. Set aside.

Now, combine guava, ginger, Swiss chard, kale, and spinach in a juicer and process until juiced.

Transfer to serving glasses and stir in the coconut water and pure coconut sugar. Optionally, top with some grated ginger.

Add some ice and serve immediately.

Nutrition information per serving: Kcal: 287, Protein: 30.8g, Carbs: 80g, Fats: 6.7g

19. Mango Lemon Juice

Ingredients:

1 cup mango, cubed

1 large lemon, peeled

1 cup fresh cherries, pitted

1 cup watermelon, cubed

1 tbsp liquid honey

2 oz water

Preparation:

Peel the mango and cut into small chunks. Set aside.

Peel the lemon and cut lengthwise in half. Set aside.

Wash the cherries under cold running water. Drain and cut in half. Remove the pits and set aside.

Cut the watermelon lengthwise. For one cup, you will need one large wedge. Peel and cut into chunks. Remove the seeds and set aside. Reserve the rest of the melon for some other juices.

Now, process mango, lemon, cherries, and watermelon in a juicer.

Transfer to serving glasses and add few ice cubes before

serving.

Enjoy!

Nutrition information per serving: Kcal: 288, Protein: 4.6g, Carbs: 68.3g, Fats: 1.3g

20. Apricot Cucumber Juice

Ingredients:

1 cup of apricots, pitted

1 large cucumber, sliced

1 large peach, pitted

1 large apple, cored

1 small ginger knob, peeled and diced

Preparation:

Wash the apricots and peach. Cut in half and remove the pit. Cut into bite-sized pieces and set aside.

Wash the cucumber and cut into thick slices. Set aside.

Wash the apple and remove the core. Cut into bite-sized pieces and set aside.

Peel the ginger and set aside.

Now, process apricots, cucumber, peach, apple, and ginger in a juicer.

Transfer to serving glasses and add some ice.

Serve immediately.

Nutrition information per serving: Kcal: 257, Protein: 6.7g, Carbs: 73.3g, Fats: 1.8g

21. Cucumber Lime Juice

Ingredients:

1 large cucumber

1 large lime, peeled

1 ripe avocado, pitted and peeled

1 large guava, peeled

2 oz coconut water

Preparation:

Wash the cucumber and cut into thick slices. Set aside. Peel the lime and cut lengthwise in half. Set aside. Peel the avocado and cut in half. Remove the pit and cut into chunks. Set aside. Peel the guava and cut into small chunks. Set aside.

Now, process cucumber, lime, avocado, and guava in a juicer.

Transfer to serving glasses and stir in the coconut water. Optionally, add a teaspoon of marmite.

Add some ice and serve immediately.

Nutrition information per serving: Kcal: 352, Protein: 7.6g, Carbs: 41.6g, Fats: 30.3g

22. Banana Apple Juice

Ingredients:

1 large banana, sliced

2 large Gala apples, cored

1 cup fresh cherries, pitted

1 cup watercress, torn

A handful of fresh spinach, torn

Preparation:

Peel the banana and cut into small chunks. Set aside. Wash the cherries under cold running water. Drain and cut in half. Remove the pits and set aside. Combine watercress and spinach in a colander and wash thoroughly. Torn with hands and set aside. Now, combine banana, apples, cherries, watercress, and spinach in a juicer and process until juiced. Transfer to serving glasses and add few ice cubes before serving.

Enjoy!

Nutritional information per serving: Kcal: 390, Protein: 6.6g, Carbs: 113g, Fats: 1.7g

23. Orange Pomegranate Juice

Ingredients:

1 large orange, peeled

1 cup pomegranate seeds

3 large carrots, sliced

1 large zucchini, peeled and cubed

1 small ginger slice, 1-inch

Preparation:

Peel the orange and divide into wedges. Set aside.

Cut the top of the pomegranate fruit using a sharp knife. Slice down to each of the white membranes inside of the fruit. Pop the seeds into a measuring cup and set aside.

Wash the carrots and cut into thick slices. Set aside.

Wash the zucchini and cut in half. Scoop out the seeds using a spoon. Cut into small chunks and set aside.

Peel the ginger knob and set aside.

Now, process orange, pomegranate seeds, carrots, zucchini, and ginger in a juicer.

Transfer to serving glasses and add some ice before serving.

Nutritional information per serving: Kcal: 239, Protein: 9.2g, Carbs: 69.7g, Fats: 2.8g

24. Coconut Pineapple Juice

Ingredients:

1 cup pineapple, chunked

¼ cup pure coconut water, unsweetened

1 whole grapefruit, peeled

1 large orange, peeled

1 cup cauliflower, chopped

Preparation:

Cut the top of a pineapple and peel it using a sharp knife. Cut into small chunks. Reserve the rest of the pineapple in a refrigerator.

Peel the grapefruit and orange and divide into wedges. Set aside.

Trim off the outer leaves of cauliflower. Wash it and cut into small pieces. Reserve the rest in the refrigerator.

Now, process pineapple, grapefruit, orange, and cauliflower in a juicer.

Transfer to serving glasses and stir in the pure coconut water. Optionally, add some cinnamon or agave nectar for extra flavor.

Add few ice cubes and serve immediately.

Nutritional information per serving: Kcal: 247, Protein: 6.5g, Carbs: 74g, Fats: 1g

25. Zucchini Watermelon Juice

Ingredients:

1 medium-sized zucchini, peeled and chopped

1 cup watermelon, diced

4 cups green grapes

1 small ginger knob, peeled

1 tbsp fresh mint, finely chopped

Preparation:

Wash the zucchini and cut in half. Scoop out the seeds using a spoon. Cut into small chunks and set aside.

Cut the watermelon lengthwise. For one cup, you will need about 1 large wedge. Peel and cut into chunks. Remove the seeds and set aside. Reserve the rest of the melon for some other juices.

Wash the grapes under cold running water. Drain and set aside.

Peel the ginger slice and set aside.

Now, process zucchini, watermelon, grapes, and ginger in a juicer.

Transfer to serving glasses and garnish with mint.

Refrigerate for 15 minutes before serving.

Nutritional information per serving: Kcal: 308, Protein: 5.7g, Carbs: 81.3g, Fats: 2.1g

26. Beet Banana Juice

Ingredients:

2 cups beets, chopped

2 cups beet greens, chopped

1 small banana, peeled

1 cup blueberries, fresh

1 tsp marmite

Preparation:

Wash the beets and separate the beet greens. Chop into small pieces and set aside.

Peel the banana and cut into chunks. Set aside.

Wash the blueberries under cold running water. Drain and set aside.

Now, process beets, beet greens, banana, and blueberries in a juicer.

Transfer to serving glasses and stir in the marmite.

Serve immediately.

Nutritional information per serving: Kcal: 252, Protein: 9.8g, Carbs: 78.4g, Fats: 1.4g

27. Cranberry Apple Juice

Ingredients:

1 cup fresh cranberries

3 small Zestar apples, cored

1 cup fresh blueberries

1 cup fresh kale, torn

1 tbsp liquid honey

Preparation:

Combine cranberries and blueberries in a colander and wash under cold running water. Drain and set aside. Wash the apples and remove the core. Cut into bite-sized pieces and set aside.

Wash the kale thoroughly and torn with hands. Set aside. Now, process cranberries, apples, blueberries, and kale in a juicer.

Transfer to serving glasses and stir in the honey. Add some ice or refrigerate before serving.

Nutrition information per serving: Kcal: 368, Protein: 5.6g, Carbs: 106g, Fats: 2.2g

28. Pineapple Cucumber Juice

Ingredients:

1 cup pineapple, chunked

1 large cucumber, sliced

1 large grapefruit, peeled

1 small Granny Smith's apple, cored

1 small ginger root slice, 1-inch

1 large lemon, peeled

Preparation:

Cut the top of a pineapple and peel it using a sharp knife. Cut into small chunks. Reserve the rest of the pineapple in a refrigerator.

Wash the cucumber and cut into thick slices. Set aside.

Peel the grapefruit and divide into wedges. Set aside.

Wash the apple and remove the core. Cut into bite-sized pieces and set aside.

Peel the ginger root slice and set aside.

Peel the lemon and cut lengthwise in half. Set aside.

Now, process pineapple, cucumber, grapefruit, apple,

ginger, and lemon in a juicer.

Transfer to serving glasses and refrigerate for 30 minutes before serving.

Enjoy!

Nutrition information per serving: Kcal: 280, Protein: 6.1g, Carbs: 84.2g, Fats: 1.3g

29. Melon Coconut Juice

Ingredients:

1 large honeydew melon wedge

2 oz coconut water

1 cup fresh strawberries

1 cup fresh mint, torn

2 medium-sized red apples, cored

¼ tsp cinnamon, ground

Preparation:

Cut the honeydew melon lengthwise in half. Scoop out the seeds using a spoon. Cut the large wedges and peel them. Cut into small chunks and place in a bowl. Wrap the rest of the melon in a plastic foil and refrigerate.

Wash the strawberries under cold running water and cut in small pieces. Set aside.

Wash the mint thoroughly and torn with hands. Set aside.

Wash the apples and remove the core. Cut into bite-sized pieces. Set aside.

Now, process honeydew melon, strawberries, mint, and apples in a juicer.

Transfer to serving glasses and stir in the coconut water and cinnamon.

Add ice cubes and serve immediately.

Nutritional information per serving: Kcal: 293, Protein: 4.5g, Carbs: 84g, Fats: 1.6g

30. Apple Green Juice

Ingredients:

2 small Zestar apples, peeled and cored

1 whole apricot, cored

1 cup collard greens, torn

¼ cup pure coconut water, unsweetened

1 tsp marmite

Preparation:

Wash the apples and remove the core. Cut into bite-sized pieces and set aside.

Wash the apricot and cut in half. Remove the pit and cut into small pieces. Set aside.

Wash the collard greens thoroughly and torn with hands. Set aside.

Now, process apples, apricot, and collard greens in a juicer.

Transfer to serving glasses and stir in the coconut water and marmite.

Add some ice before serving and enjoy!

Nutritional information per serving: Kcal: 154, Protein: 3g, Carbs: 47.9g, Fats: 0.9g

31. Spicy Cantaloupe Juice

Ingredients:

1 cup cantaloupe, diced

2 cups mustard greens, torn

1 whole grapefruit, peeled

4 cups parsley, chopped

¼ tsp cayenne pepper, ground

¼ tsp salt

¼ cup water

Preparation:

Cut the cantaloupe in half. Scoop out the seeds and flesh. Cut two wedges and peel them. Chop into chunks and set aside. Reserve the rest of the cantaloupe in a refrigerator.

Wash the mustard greens and parsley. Torn with hands and set aside.

Peel the grapefruit and divide into wedges. Set aside.

Now, process cantaloupe, mustard greens, grapefruit, and parsley in a juicer.

Transfer to serving glasses and stir in the water, cayenne, and salt.

Add some ice and serve immediately.

Nutritional information per serving: Kcal: 207, Protein: 13.5g, Carbs: 59.5g, Fats: 3g

32. Grapefruit Lime Juice

Ingredients:

1 whole grapefruit, peeled

1 whole lime, peeled

2 cups cherries, without pits

1 tbsp fresh mint, chopped

1 oz coconut water

Preparation:

Peel the grapefruit and divide into wedges. Set aside.

Peel the lime and cut lengthwise in half. Set aside.

Wash the cherries under cold running water. Cut in half and remove the pits. Set aside.

Now, process grapefruit, lime, and cherries in a juicer. Transfer to serving glasses and stir in the coconut water.

Garnish with fresh mint and serve immediately.

Enjoy!

Nutritional information per serving: Kcal: 276, Protein: 5.8g, Carbs: 84.4g, Fats: 3.1g

33. Plum Cucumber Juice

Ingredients:

1 cup fresh plums, pitted

1 large cucumber, sliced

2 cups green grapes

1 cup mustard greens, torn

1 small ginger root slice, peeled

Preparation:

Wash the plums and cut in half. Remove the pits and set aside.

Wash the cucumber and cut into thick slices. Set aside.

Rinse the grapes under cold running water. Drain and fill the measuring cup. Reserve the rest in the refrigerator.

Wash the mustard greens thoroughly and torn with hands. Set aside.

Peel the ginger root slice and set aside.

Now, process plums, cucumber, grapes, mustard greens, and ginger in a juicer.

Transfer to serving glasses and refrigerate for 20 minutes before serving.

Enjoy!

Nutrition information per serving: Kcal: 339, Protein: 6.9g, Carbs: 56.7g, Fats: 21.9g

34. Watermelon Lime Juice

Ingredients:

1 cup watermelon, diced

1 whole lime, peeled

1 cup watercress, chopped

1 small ginger slice, peeled

1 cup blueberries

Preparation:

Cut the watermelon lengthwise. For one cup, you will need about one large wedge. Peel and cut into chunks. Remove the seeds and set aside. Reserve the rest of for some other juices.

Peel the lime and cut lengthwise in half. Set aside.

Rinse the watercress thoroughly and roughly chop it. Set aside.

Peel the ginger slice and set aside.

Wash the blueberries under cold running water and set aside.

Now, process watermelon, lime, watercress, ginger, and blueberries in a juicer.

Transfer to serving glasses and add some ice before serving.

Enjoy!

Nutritional information per serving: Kcal: 129, Protein: 3g, Carbs: 37.4g, Fats: 0.8g

35. Cucumber Cantaloupe Juice

Ingredients:

1 large cucumber, sliced

1 cup cantaloupe, peeled and cubed

1 large mango, chopped

1 tsp marmite

2 tbsp fresh mint

Preparation:

Wash the cucumber and cut into thick slices. Set aside.

Cut the cantaloupe in half. Scoop out the seeds and flesh. Cut two wedges and peel them. Chop into chunks and set aside. Reserve the rest of the cantaloupe in a refrigerator.

Wash the mango and cut into bite-sized pieces. Set aside.

Now, process cucumber, cantaloupe, and mango in a juicer.

Transfer to serving glasses and stir in the marmite. Add few ice cubes before serving.

Garnish with mint leaves and enjoy!

Nutrition information per serving: Kcal: 268, Protein: 6.1g, Carbs: 74.4g, Fats: 1.9g

36. Apricot Cucumber Juice

Ingredients:

2 large apricots, pitted

1 large cucumber, sliced

2 large pears, cored

1 cup fresh watercress

1 cup collard greens

1 large lemon, peeled

Preparation:

Wash the apricots and cut in half. Remove the pits and chop into small pieces. Set aside.

Wash the cucumber and cut into thick slices. Set aside.

Wash the pears and remove the core. Cut into bite-sized pieces and set aside.

Combine watercress and collard greens in a colander and wash under cold running water. Drain and set aside.

Peel the lemon and cut lengthwise in half. Set aside.

Now, combine apricots, cucumber, pears, watercress, collard greens and lemon in a juicer. Process until well juiced.

Transfer to serving glasses and add some ice before serving.

Nutrition information per serving: Kcal: 293, Protein: 7.1g, Carbs: 96.1g, Fats: 1.7g

37. Green Apple Juice

Ingredients:

1 large Granny Smith's apple, cored

1 cup fennel, chopped

1 cup collard greens, torn

1 large leek, chopped

1 cup fresh mint, torn

A handful of spinach

1 tbsp liquid honey

1 tsp marmite

Preparation:

Wash the apple and cut in half. Remove the core and cut into bite-sized pieces. Set aside.

Wash the fennel bulb and trim off the wilted outer layers. Cut into small chunks and fill the measuring cup. Reserve the rest in the refrigerator.

In a large colander, combine collard greens, mint, and spinach. Rinse thoroughly under cold running water and drain. Torn with hands and set aside.

Wash the leek and cut into bite-sized pieces. Set aside.

Now, combine apple, fennel, collard greens, mint, spinach, and leek in a juicer. Process until well juiced.

Transfer to a serving glass and serve immediately.

Nutritional information per serving: Kcal: 190, Protein: 6.9g, Carbs: 56.7g, Fats: 1.4g

38. Cucumber Beet Juice

Ingredients:

1 cup cucumber, sliced

1 cup beets, sliced

1 cup blackberries

1 whole lemon, peeled

1 oz coconut water

Preparation:

Wash the cucumber and cut into thin slices. Fill the measuring cup and reserve the rest in the refrigerator for some other juice.

Wash the beets and trim off the green parts. Cut into bite-sized pieces and fill the measuring cup. Reserve the rest for later.

Using a small colander, rinse the blackberries under cold running water. Slightly drain and set aside.

Peel the lemon and cut lengthwise in half. Set aside.

Now, combine cucumber, beets, blackberries, and lemon in a juicer and process until juiced. Transfer to a serving glass and stir in the coconut water. Add some ice and serve immediately.

Nutritional information per serving: Kcal: 103, Protein: 5.2g, Carbs: 34.2g, Fats: 1.2g

39. Apricot Carrot Juice

Ingredients:

1 cup apricots, sliced

1 medium-sized carrot, sliced

1 cup raspberries

2 whole plums, pitted

1 tbsp honey, raw

Preparation:

Wash the apricots and cut lengthwise in half. Remove the pits and cut into thin slices. Fill the measuring cup and reserve the rest for later.

Wash and peel the carrot. Cut into thin slices and set aside.

Using a colander, wash the raspberries in under cold running water. Slightly drain and set aside.

Wash the plums and cut in half. Remove the pits and set aside.

Now, combine apricots, carrot, raspberries, and plums in a juicer and process until well juiced.

Transfer to a serving glass and stir in the honey. Add some crushed ice before serving.

Nutritional information per serving: Kcal: 232, Protein: 5.3g, Carbs: 70.9g, Fats: 1.9g

40. Artichoke Cucumber Juice

Ingredients:

1 medium-sized artichoke, chopped

1 cup cucumber, sliced

1 cup fennel, chopped

1 medium-sized carrot, sliced

¼ tsp turmeric, ground

Preparation:

Trim off the outer leaves of the artichoke using a sharp paring knife. Wash it and cut into bite-sized pieces. Set aside.

Wash and peel the cucumber. Cut into thin slices and fill the measuring cup. Refrigerate the rest for later.

Wash the fennel bulb and trim off the wilted outer layers. Cut into small pieces and fill the measuring cup. Reserve the rest for some other juice.

Wash and peel the carrot. Cut into thin slices and set aside.

Now, combine artichoke, cucumber, fennel, and carrot in a juicer a process until well juiced.

Transfer to a serving glass and stir in the turmeric. Add

some ice and serve immediately.

Nutritional information per serving: Kcal: 73, Protein: 6.1g, Carbs: 27.5g, Fats: 0.6g

41. Zucchini Beet Juice

Ingredients:

1 small zucchini, chopped

1 medium-sized beet, trimmed and chopped

1 large red bell pepper, chopped

1 whole leek, chopped

1 tsp apple cider vinegar

¼ tsp salt

Preparation:

Peel the zucchini and cut into bite-sized pieces. Set aside.

Wash the beets and trim off the green ends. Peel and cut into small pieces. Set aside.

Wash the bell pepper and cut lengthwise in half. Remove the seeds and cut into small pieces. Set aside.

Wash the leek and cut into bite-sized pieces. Set aside.

Now, combine zucchini, beet, bell pepper, and leek in a juicer. Process until juiced. Transfer to a serving glass and stir in the salt and vinegar.

Refrigerate for 15 minutes before serving.

Enjoy!

Nutritional information per serving: Kcal: 126, Protein: 5.7g, Carbs: 34g, Fats: 1.3g

42. Banana Melon Juice

Ingredients:

1 large banana, sliced

1 honeydew melon wedge, peeled

1 large grapefruit, wedged

1 whole lime, peeled

1 small mandarin orange, wedged

1 tbsp liquid honey

Preparation:

Peel the banana and cut into thin slices. Set aside.

Cut one large honeydew melon wedge and peel it. Remove the seeds and cut into bite-sized pieces. Set aside.

Peel the grapefruit and divide into wedges. Cut each wedge in half and set aside.

Peel the lime and cut lengthwise in half. Set aside.

Peel the mandarin orange and divide into wedges. Set aside.

Now, combine banana, melon, grapefruit, lime, and orange in a juicer and process until juiced.

Transfer to a serving glass and stir in the liquid honey. Add some ice before serving enjoy!

Nutritional information per serving: Kcal: 281, Protein: 5.2g, Carbs: 83.6g, Fats: 1.2g

43. Orange Mint Juice

Ingredients:

1 large orange, peeled

1 cup fresh mint, torn

1 cup cantaloupe, chopped

1 cup blackberries

¼ tsp cinnamon, ground

Preparation:

Peel the orange and divide into wedges. Cut each wedge in half and set aside.

Rinse the mint under cold running water and drain. Torn into small pieces and set aside.

Cut the cantaloupe in half. Scrape out the seeds and cut one large wedge. Peel and chop into small pieces. Fill the measuring cup and wrap the rest in a plastic foil. Refrigerate for later.

Place the blackberries in a colander and rinse well. Drain and set aside.

Now, combine orange, mint, cantaloupe, and blackberries in a juicer and process until juiced. Transfer to a serving glass and stir in the cinnamon.

Add some ice and serve immediately.

Nutrition information per serving: Kcal: 157, Protein: 5.9g, Carbs: 51.9g, Fats: 1.5g

44. Black Grape Banana Juice

Ingredients:

1 cup black grapes

1 large banana, peeled

2 cups blueberries

1 cup fresh mint, torn

2 tbsp coconut water

¼ tsp cinnamon, ground

Preparation:

Rinse the grapes and remove the stems. Fill the measuring cup and reserve the rest in the refrigerator. Set aside.

Peel the banana and cut into thick slices. Set aside.

Place the blueberries in a colander. Rinse well under cold running water and drain. Set aside.

Rinse the mint thoroughly under cold running water. Drain and torn into small pieces. Set aside.

Now, combine grapes, banana, blueberries, and mint in a juicer and process until juiced. Transfer to a serving glass and stir in the coconut water and cinnamon.

Refrigerate for 15 minutes before serving.

Nutrition information per serving: Kcal: 326, Protein: 6.2g, Carbs: 93.4g, Fats: 2.1g

45. Beet Zestar Juice

Ingredients:

1 cup beets, sliced

1 small Zestar apple, cored

1 cup fresh kale, torn

1 cup cantaloupe, cubed

¼ tsp ginger, ground

Preparation:

Wash the beets and trim off the green ends. Cut into thin slices and fill the measuring cup. Reserve the rest for some other juice.

Wash the apple and cut lengthwise in half. Remove the core and cut into bite-sized pieces. Set aside.

Rinse the kale thoroughly under cold running water. Drain and torn into small pieces. Set aside.

Cut the cantaloupe in half. Scrape out the seeds and cut one large wedge. Peel and chop into small pieces. Fill the measuring cup and wrap the rest in a plastic foil. Refrigerate for later.

Now, combine beets, apple, kale, and cantaloupe in a juicer

and process until juiced. Transfer to a serving glass and stir in the ginger.

Add some ice and serve immediately.

Nutrition information per serving: Kcal: 181, Protein: 7g, Carbs: 51.1g, Fats: 1.4g

JUICE RECIPES

1. Walnutty Bread-a-licious

Ingredients:

1 tbsp of honey

½ cup of ground walnuts

2 cups of almond flour

1 tbsp of vanilla extract

1 cup of sour cream

½ tsp of sea salt

1 teaspoon of baking soda

2 tbsp of coconut oil

Preparation:

Put the honey, sour cream, walnuts and vanilla extract in the food processor and mix well for 40 seconds.

Pour the mixture in a bowl and add flour, baking soda, and salt. Stir well with a fork or even better with an electric mixer to get a smooth dough.

Pour the coconut oil over a baking sheet. Preheat the oven

to 250 degrees. It takes about 40 minutes for bread to start rising. When it does, remove it from the oven and let it stand for at least 2 hours before eating.

The sweet taste of this bread is perfect for breakfast.

Nutrition information per serving: Kcal: 90 Protein: 1.1g, Carbs: 11.2g, Fats: 4.2g

2. Almond-Packed pancakes

Ingredients:

1 cup of almond flour

½ cup of minced almonds

½ cup of milk

1 cup of almond milk

½ cup of water

Salt

A dash of cinnamon

1 tbsp of olive oil

Preparation:

Make a smooth dough with almond flour, almonds, milk, almond milk, salt and water, using an electric mixer. Add some cinnamon for flavor – ¼ tsp will do the job. Fry over a medium heat for about 3-4 minutes on each side, or until nice light brown color. Depending on your taste, you can top them with strawberry syrup, fresh blueberries, banana slices, etc.

Nutrition information per serving: Kcal: 150 Protein: 6.3g, Carbs: 4.4g, Fats: 13.5g

3. Peanut butter oats

Ingredients:

1 cup of amaranth, cooked

1 cup of unsweetened almond milk

2 tbsp of organic peanut butter

1 tbsp of strawberry syrup

1 tsp of cinnamon

Preparation:

Place the ingredients in a bowl and stir well until you get a nice, smooth mixture. If necessary, add some water. Pour this mixture in a tall glasses and leave in the refrigerator overnight.

Nutrition information per serving: Kcal: 278 Protein: 10.3g, Carbs: 35.5g, Fats: 10.2g

4. Pineapple omelet with almonds

Ingredients:

3 thick slices of pineapple, peeled

2 eggs

½ cup of almonds, minced

½ tsp of sea salt

Preparation:

Break the eggs into a bowl and beat well until combined. Add minced almonds and mix well. Season with salt.

Use a non-stick frying pan. Fist you want to fry pineapple slices for about 2-3 minutes on each side, until nicely golden brown color. Reduce the heat to low. Pour egg mixture into pan and fry for few more minutes, stirring constantly. Remove from the heat and enjoy.

Nutrition information per serving: Kcal: 185 Protein: 4.4g, Carbs: 4.8g, Fats: 10.3g

5. Avocado sandwich

Ingredients:

2 thick slices of avocado, pitted

½ cup of button mushrooms, fresh

4 leaves of lettuce, washed

Preparation:

Heat up a non-stick frying pan (you can also use a grill pan). Slice the button mushrooms in half and add to the saucepan. Cook for about 3-4 minutes, over a medium heat, until all the water evaporates. Remove from the saucepan and allow it to cool for a while. Use avocado slices to prepare a tasty sandwich.

Nutrition information per serving: Kcal: 296 Protein: 14g, Carbs: 36.1g, Fats: 16.4g

6. Coconut milk pancakes with strawberries

Ingredients:

1 glass of coconut milk

2 eggs, beaten

½ cup of whipped cream

1 glass of water

½ tsp of salt

1 cup of buckwheat flour

½ cup of ground walnuts

½ cup of strawberries, chopped

Olive oil

Preparation:

Mix well coconut milk, eggs, whipped cream and water in a large bowl, using an electric mixer. Add flour and salt and mix well with a stick blender to get a smooth dough. Now you want to add ground walnuts. Heat up the oil over a medium temperature. Make a pancakes with ¼ cup of dough. Fry in hot oil until gold brown on both sides. Top with strawberries.

Nutrition information per serving: Kcal: 630 Protein: 23.4g, Carbs: 86.1g, Fats: 22.5g

7. Crunchy almond delight

Ingredients:

1 cup of Greek yogurt

½ cup of frozen blueberries

¼ cup of whole almonds

1 tbsp of sugar

Preparation:

Combine the ingredients in a blender and mix for 30 seconds. Pour the mixture into tall glass and leave in the freezer for about an hour.

Nutrition information per serving: Kcal: 289 Protein: 11.6g, Carbs: 46.3g, Fats: 7.9g

8. Banana pancakes

Ingredients:

1 cup of sliced banana

½ cup of rice flower

½ cup of skim milk

½ cup of almond milk

3 tbsp of brown sugar

1 tsp of vanilla extract

2 eggs

1 tbsp Olive Oil

Preparation:

Combine banana slices, rice flour, skim milk and almond milk in a bowl and mix with an electric mixer until smooth mixture. Cover it and let it stand for 15 minutes.

In another bowl, mix the almond cream with sugar, vanilla extract and eggs. Beat well with a fork, or even better with an electric mixer. You want to get a foamy mixture. Set aside.

Pour some olive oil on a frying pan. Use ¼ cup of banana mixture to make one pancake. Fry your pancakes for about

2-3 minutes on each side. This mixture should give you 8 pancakes.

Spread 1 tbsp of almond cream mixture over each pancake and serve.

Nutrition information per serving: Kcal: 276 Protein: 4.2g, Carbs: 55.8g, Fats: 2.9g

9. Quinoa smoothie

Ingredients:

1 cup of quinoa, cooked

1 banana

½ cup of strawberries

1 cup of low fat yogurt

1 cup of skim milk

1 tsp of ground vanilla sticks

1 tsp of honey

Preparation:

Combine the ingredients in a blender and mix for few minutes, until smooth mixture. Allow it to cool in the refrigerator for a while.

Nutrition information per serving: Kcal: 151 Protein: 3.1g, Carbs: 35.4g, Fats: 1.8g

10. Easy Beef Burritos

Ingredients:

2 pounds of skirt steak

1 medium-sized onion, finely chopped

4 garlic cloves, crushed

1 medium sized green chile pepper, diced

5oz hot pepper sauce

1 tsp of salt

½ tbsp of Cayenne pepper

1 tbsp parsley, finely chopped

3 tbsp extra virgin olive oil

Other:

10 flour tortillas

2 ripe tomatoes, sliced

10 Iceberg lettuce leaves, shredded

1 cup of grated Cheddar cheese

¾ cup of sweet corn

Preparation:

Heat up the olive oil in a large skillet, over a medium-high heat. Briefly brown the meat on both sides and remove from the heat. Transfer to a slow cooker and add finely chopped onion, crushed garlic, parsley, and diced chili pepper. Season with salt, Cayenne pepper, and add hot pepper sauce. Add enough water to cover ½ of the roast – about 3 cups. Reduce the heat to low, cover, and cook for about 5 hours. Check occasionally to make sure there is enough water. After 5 hours, remove the lid and continue to cook until all the water evaporates. Remove from the heat and cool for a while. Using a sharp knife, thinly slice the meat and transfer to a plate.

Heat the tortillas in the microwave for about one minute. Spread some meat on each tortilla, add sliced tomato, lettuce, sweet corn and Cheddar.

Serving tip:

Sprinkle some ground chili, garlic powder, Cayenne pepper, or some other spice before serving.

Nutrition information per serving: Kcal: 431 Protein: 26.9g, Carbs: 33.4g, Fats: 20g

11. Chicken and Black Beans Tacos

1 ½ pounds of chicken breast, boneless and skinless

2 ripe tomatoes, peeled and sliced

2 garlic cloves, crushed

½ cup finely chopped celery

2 tbsp tomato paste

¼ cup of fresh lime juice

½ tsp of salt

2 tsp of Cayenne pepper

¼ tsp of black pepper, ground

2 tbsp extra virgin olive oil

Other:

1 (15oz) can black beans, rinsed

1 medium-sized onion, finely chopped

1 cup of lettuce, shredded

1 large tomato, finely chopped

1 (7oz) can green salsa

½ tsp chili powder

½ tsp of salt

6 taco shells

2 tbsp extra virgin olive oil

Preparation:

Combine the tomatoes, garlic, celery, tomato paste, lime juice, salt, cayenne pepper, black pepper, and olive oil in a slow cooker. Place the chicken meat on top and add enoug water to cover 1/3 of the meat. Set the heat to low, cover, and cook for 3 hours, or until the meat is tender. Check often to make sure that there is enough water in your slow cooker.

When the meat softens, remove the lid and set the heat to high. Cook until the water evaporates. Remove from the heat and chill.

Finely chop the chicken breasts – into bite-sized pieces. Set aside.

Heat up the remaining two tablespoons of olive oil in a medium-sized skillet. Add finely chopped onion and stir-fry until translucent. Stir in black beans, green salsa, chili powder, and salt. Reduce the heat to minimum and simmer for about ten minutes, until the mixture thickens.

Serve the green salsa mixture with meat, taco shells, chopped tomato, and lettuce.

Useful tip:

If you're in a hurry, set the cooker's heat to high and reduce the cooking time to 1 hour.

Nutrition information per serving: Kcal: 266 Protein: 28.8g, Carbs: 11.8g, Fats: 11g

12. Garlic chicken breast

Ingredients:

6 pounds chicken breast

1 ½ cups chicken broth

1/8 tablespoon pepper

2 minced garlic cloves

½ tablespoon garlic powder

Preparation:

Starting off with a fairly simple recipe, take the slow cooker and put the chicken breast in it. Next, add the broth, garlic powder and pepper to the chicken breast. On top of the breast, sprinkle the minced garlic cloves. Set the heat to low and cook for 4 to 6 hours. You can also lower the setting to warm and cook the chicken breast for 8 hours. In both cases, the recipe remains the same.

Nutrition information per serving: Kcal: 199 Protein: 18.6g, Carbs: 2g, Fats: 12.8g

13. Chia seeds – indian way

Ingredients:

1 cup of chia seeds

1 cup of low fat cream

2 cloves of garlic, chopped

1 tsp of ground ginger

¼ tsp of salt

2 small chili peppers

1 small onion, chopped

Preparation:

Use 3 cups of water and bring it to boil. Put chia seeds in it and cook it for 30 minutes on a low temperature. When tender, add spices and mix well. Cook for about 5-10 minutes on a low temperature, stirring constantly. Top with low fat cream.

Nutrition information per serving: Kcal: 211 Protein: 9.6g, Carbs: 18.6g, Fats: 14.1g

14. Chickpea & chili soup

Ingredients:

2 tsp of cumin seeds

½ cup of chili flakes

½ cup of lentils

1 tbsp of olive oil

1 red onion, chopped

3 cups of vegetable stock

1 cup of can tomatoes, whole or chopped

½ cup of chickpeas

Bunch of coriander, roughly chopped

4 tbsp of Greek yogurt, for serving

Preparation:

Heat-up a large frying pan over a medium heat. And add cumin seeds and chili flakes. Briefly cook for about a minute. Reduce the heat and add the onion, lentils, stock, and tomatoes. Cook for 15 minutes, or until lentils are tender.

Transfer to a food processor and blend until puree. Remove from the food processor and pour the soup back into the pan. Now add chickpeas and heat up.

Season with salt and pepper and add coriander. Top with some yogurt before serving.

Nutrition information per serving: Kcal: 244 Protein: 14.2g, Carbs: 37.6g, Fats: 5.1g

15. Fresh legumes – mexican way

Ingredients:

1 ½ cups of fresh legumes, chopped

1 ½ tbs of red chili powder or one tbs of Cayenne pepper

1 ½ tbs of onion flakes or 1 tbs of onion powder

¾ tsp of oregano

¾ tsp of garlic powder

¾ tsp of ground cumin

¾ tsp of salt

3 cups of water to start (add more throughout the cooking process)

Preparation:

It is best to soak the legumes the night before. Wash them in a colander and then put them in a saucepan and cover them with plenty of water and let soak for 24 hours. Then drain the legumes. In a large skillet, spread the legumes out and add three cups of water. Add the recipe spices and cook over a medium heat until legumes are soft enough that they can be mashed. You will need to add more water during the cooking process as your legumes will continue to absorb it. Add water a half-cup at a time, just enough to keep the mixture moist with some visible liquid. The entire cooking process will take about 45 minutes. Legumes will be soft to chew. Mash after cooking if preferred.

Nutrition information per serving: Kcal: 500 Protein: 38.6g, Carbs: 98.6g, Fats: 1.9g

16. Southwest Chicken Chili

Ingredients:

4 (4oz) chicken breast halves

1 (15oz) can pinto beans

3 large tomatoes, peeled and finely chopped

1 medium-sized green pepper, sliced

1 cup of chopped onions

2 garlic cloves, crushed

2 tbsp cormeal

2 tsp of ground cumin

1 tbsp of chili powder

¼ cup of shredded Cheddar

2 tbsp vegetable oil

½ tsp of salt

Preparation:

Heat up the oil in a skillet, over medium heat. Add chopped onios and garlic. Stir-fry until translucet. Remove from the heat and transfer to a deep pot.

In a large bowl, combine cornmeal with cumin, chili, and

salt. Place the meat in the bowl and toss well to coat. Transfer to the pot.

Add the remaining ingredients and one cup of water. Cover and set the heat to low. Cook for 50 minutes.

Nutrition information per serving: Kcal: 284 Protein: 29.3g, Carbs: 21.8g, Fats: 4.1g

17. Tex Mex Chicken

Ingredients:

1 pound of chicnek breast, boneless and skinless, shredded into large pieces

1 cup of dried pinto beans

1 cup of frozen corn

2 red peppers, sliced

2 spring onions, sliced

2 tbsp all-purpose flour

1 cup of medium salsa

½ tsp of salt

1 tbsp of Cayenne pepper

1 cup of sour cream

¼ cup of fresh parsley, finely chopped

Preparation:

Combine the beans, sliced peppers, spring onions, flour, and salsa in a pressure cooker.

Season the meat with salt and cayenne and place on top of vegetable mixture. Add enough water to cover 1/3 of the mixture.

Cover the slow cooker and set the heat on low. Cook for 1 hour.

Serve with two tablespoons of sour cream and chopped parsley.

Make it different:

Preheat the oven to 350 degrees. After the meat has soften in a pressure cooker, transfer everything in oven-proof dish. Bake for 30 more minutes, or until the meat is lightly carred and crispy. Serve with sour cream and parsley.

Nutrition information per serving: Kcal: 408 Protein: 42.9g, Carbs: 18.3g, Fats: 18.6g

18. Mexican Beef, Rice 'n' Beans Bake

Ingredients:

2 pounds of lean ground beef

1 cup of long grain rice

15oz black beans, cooked

15oz fire-roasted tomatoes

½ cup sweet corn

1 green pepper, finely chopped

1 red pepper, finely chopped

2 medium-sized onions, peeled and finely chopped

2 cups of chicken broth

1 tsp of salt

1 tbsp chili powder

2 tbsp vegetable oil

¼ cup fresh parsley, finely chopped

½ cup sour cream

Preparation:

Heat up the oil over a medium-high heat, in a large skillet.

Add the onions and stir-fry until translucent. Now add green pepper, red pepper, and ground beef. Stir well to combine and continue to cook for about five minutes. Transfer to a deep pot.

Add the remaining ingredients and cover. Cook for about an hour over a medium-low heat.

Top with sour cream and fresh parsley before serving.

Nutrition information per serving: Kcal: 384 Protein: 19.1g, Carbs: 40.3g, Fats: 16.7g

19. Beef sandwiches au jus

Ingredients:

2 pounds beef rump roast

1 tsp of garlic powder

1 tsp of rosemary powder

2 tsp of sugar

1 ½ cup of fresh apple juice

2 cups of beef broth

½ tsp chili powder

6 buns

Preparation:

Combine the apple juice, beef broth, garlic powder, rosemary powder, chili powder, and sugar in a medium-sized bowl. Stir well to combine.

Place the meat in a deep pot and pour the apple mixture over it. Set the heat to low, cover and cook until tender.

After about an hour, remove the meat from the pot. Keep the liquid. Using a sharp knife, thinly slice the meat and divide between six buns. Serve with wine-based liquid for dipping.

Serving tip:

Serve with sliced pickles or fresh lettuce.

Nutrition information per serving: Kcal: 420 Protein: 42.2g, Carbs: 27.1g, Fats: 16.4g

20. Beef Stroganoff

Ingredients:

2 pounds of stew beef

2 tbsp of olive oil

2 large onions, finely chopped

1 garlic clove, crushed

1 cup of button mushrooms, sliced

½ cup of Gorgonzola, chopped

1 ½ cup of sour cream

½ tsp of salt

½ tsp of pepper

¼ cup of water

3 cups of cooked rice

Preparation:

Combine the ingredients, except the sour cream, in a slow cooker. Cover and set on low for 3 hours.

If you set the heat on high, you can reduce the cooking time to 1 hour.

When done, stir in sour cream and serve.

Nutrition information per serving: Kcal: 330 Protein: 19.9g, Carbs: 22.7g, Fats: 18.4g

21. Hamburger Soup

Ingredients:

1 pound of lean ground beef

1 large onion, peeled and sliced

2 cups of cooked green beans

2 large carrots, sliced

2 medium-sized potatoes, chopped

2 large tomatoes, peeled and finely chopped

1 tbsp of tomato paste

3 cups of water

1 tsp of salt

½ tsp of pepper

2 tbsp of vegetable oil

Preparation:

Heat up the oil in a large skillet over a medium-high heat. Add the chopped onion and stir-fry for a couple of minutes, or until translucent. Now add the ground beef, salt, and pepper. Continue to cook until the beef is evenly brown. Remove from the heat and transfer to a heavy bottomed pot.

Add sliced potatoes, green beans, carrots, chopped tomatoes, and one tablespoon of tomato paste. Pour the water over the vegetables and cover. Cook for about 45 minutes over medium-high heat.

Nutrition information per serving: Kcal: 165 Protein: 13.9g, Carbs: 14.8g, Fats: 6.5g

22. Broccoli and Beef Pasta Bake

Ingredients:

14oz lean ground beef

17oz dried pasta

12 oz broccoli, sliced

½ cup tomato paste

1 tbsp sugar

1 tsp dry oregano

½ tsp salt

¼ cup olive oil

½ cup of Cheddar cheese, grated

Preparation:

Combine the tomato paste with sugar, oregano, and 4 tbsp of olive oil. Stir well.

Heat up the remaining olive oil over a medium-high heat. Add ground beef, season with some salt, and cook until brown, stirring constantly. Remove from the heat. Place sliced broccoli at the bottom of a deep pot. Than add dried pasta, ground beef, and tomato paste mixture.

Cover and cook until pasta is tender. Remove from the heat

and spread the grated Cheddar. Cover again and allow the cheese to melt.

Serve warm.

Serving tip:

Top with sour cream or Greek yogurt.

Nutrition information per serving: Kcal: 342 Protein: 28.4g, Carbs: 37.3g, Fats: 8.8g

23. Baked Ziti

Ingredients:

1 box (16oz) ziti pasta

4 large ripe tomatoes, peeled and roughly chopped

3 garlic cloves, crushed

1 tsp dry oregano

2 tsp sugar

½ cup fresh apple juice

½ tsp salt

3 tbsp olive oil

Preparation:

Heat the olive oil over a medium heat and add garlic. Briefly stir-fry and add tomatoes, oregano, sugar, salt, and butter. Stir well and reduce the heat. Cook until the tomatoes soften. Transfer to a deep pot and top with ziti. Add apple juice and one cup of water.

Cook until ziti softens.

Nutrition information per serving: Kcal: 316 Protein: 19.4g, Carbs: 30.8g, Fats: 12.9g

24. Chicken Scallopini in a Creamy Sauce

Ingredients:

2 chicken brest halves, boneless and skinless

¼ cup of butter

1 garlic clove, crushed

1 tsp of dry oregano

¼ cup of fresh lime juice

1 cup of button mushrooms, sliced

½ cup of Gorgonzola cheese, chopped

1 cup of sour cream

3 tbsp of Parmesan cheese, grated

½ tsp of salt

½ cup of all-purpose flour

1 tbsp of sugar

½ cup of sherry vinegar

Preparation:

In a small bowl, combine the flour with sour cream, sugar, Parmesan cheese, and Gorgonzola. Add fresh lime juice and beat well with electric mixer, on high.

Season each chicken breast half with salt and oregano. Place in a large skillet. Add the creamy mixture, wine, mushrooms, and garlic.

Cook for about 30 minutes, stirring constantly.

Nutrition information per serving: Kcal: 499 Protein: 17.9g, Carbs: 33.7g, Fats: 32.1g

25. Chicken Divan

Ingredients:

2 chicken breast halves, cubed

14oz broccoli, shredded

1 tsp ground ginger

2 tbsp olive oil

1 cup sour cream

2 green onions, finely chopped

2 garlic cloves, crushed

½ cup grated Parmesan

½ cup bread crumbs

½ cup of water

1 tsp of salt

Preparation:

In a bowl, combine one cup of sour cream with garlic, Parmesan, bread crumbs, ginger, and water. Stir well to combine. Add two tablespoons of olive oil and mix again.

Place the ingredients in a pressure cooker and cook for 30 minutes.

Nutrition information per serving: Kcal: 244 Protein: 18.3g, Carbs: 14.7g, Fats: 13.1g

26. Pressure Cooker's Honey Garlic Chicken

Ingredients:

1 pound chicken breast, boneless and skinless

1 ½ cups chicken broth

½ tbsp freshly ground black pepper

2 garlic cloves, crushed

½ tbsp garlic powder

Preparation:

Take the pressure cooker and put the chicken breast in it. Next, add the broth, garlic powder and pepper. Toss in the garlic cloves.

Securely lock the lid and cook for 25 minutes on high.

Nutrition information per serving: Kcal: 326 Protein: 32.5g, Carbs: 39.9g, Fats: 14.8g

27. Sticky BBQ Chicken Legs

Ingredients:

2 pounds chicken thighs, with skin and bones

1 tablespoon chilipowder

1 tbsp of fresh basil, finely chopped

¼ tsp of black pepper, freshly ground

½ tsp of sea salt

1 cup of coconut water

1 tbsp grated ginger, fresh

1 tbsp coriander seeds

2 garlic cloves, crushed

Preparation:

Put the chicken thighs along with garlic in a deep pot. Add other spices, sprinkling them evenly over the chicken thighs.

Pour in the coconut water and add the fresh basil.

Cover the pot and cook for about 40 minutes over medium heat.

After about 40 minutes, remove the lid and turn off the

heat. Allow the liquid to evaporate.

Nutrition information per serving: Kcal: 170 Protein: 18.4g, Carbs: 1.1g, Fats: 10g

28. Cheesy Chicken and Potatoes

Ingredients:

2 pieces of chicken breast, halved

3 medium-sized potatoes, sliced

1 cup of sour cream

¼ cup of Parmesan cheese

¼ cup of grated Cheddar

2 tbsp of Greek yogurt

1 tsp of rosemary powder

½ tsp of salt

1 tbsp of olive oil

¼ tbsp of Cayenne pepper

Preparation:

Add the sliced potatoes in the slow cooker. Make sure to cover the bottom.

Season the meat with salt and place in a slow cooker. In a bowl, combine the sour cream, Parmesan, Cheddar, Greek yogurt, olive oil, rosemary powder, and Cayenne pepepr. Beat well with an electric mixer on high.

Pour the cheese mixture over the meat and cover. Set for 8 hours on low heat.

Nutrition information per serving: Kcal: 290 Protein: 14.5g, Carbs: 34.5g, Fats: 11.3g

29. Glazed Salmon with Roasted Broccolini and Asparagus

Ingredients:

4 (6 oz.) fresh salmon fillets (boneless and skinless)

For the marinade

¼ cup of coconut aminos

½ teaspoon of ginger powder

2 garlic cloves, minced

½ teaspoon of salt

½ teaspoon of crushed black pepper

For the Vegetables

½ pound of broccolini, trimmed

½ pound of asparagus, trimmed

2 tablespoons of ghee

1 tablespoon of organic lemon juice

3 crushed garlic cloves

A pinch of salt and crushed black pepper

Preparation:

Preheat the oven to 400°F, lightly grease a baking dish with ghee and set aside.

Combine together all marinade ingredients in a bowl and mix until well combined.

Place the fillets on the prepared baking dish and pour with marinade to cover the fillets. Set aside.

Add all ingredients for the vegetables and toss to coat evenly with the flavouring ingredients. Transfer vegetables on a baking tray. Roast fillets together with the vegetables in a separate tray for 15 to 20 minutes. Baste the fish with marinade every 5 minutes of roasting time. Remove from the oven and set aside. Roast the vegetables until soft and cooked through, remove from the oven and transfer to a serving platter.

Top vegetables with roasted salmon and serve warm.

Nutrition information per serving: Kcal: 360 Protein: 27.1g, Carbs: 23.7g, Fats: 17.8g

30. Greek Meatballs with Avocado Tzatziki Sauce

Ingredients:

For the Meatballs

1 pound ground grass-fed beef

1 small red onion, minced

1 teaspoons minced garlic

½ organic lemon, zested

1 teaspoon of dried oregano

½ teaspoon cumin powder

½ teaspoon of coriander powder

A pinch of sea salt and pepper

For the Sauce

1 avocado, pitted and diced

1 small cucumber, seeded and diced

1 teaspoon of minced garlic

1 tablespoon of minced red onion

1 organic lemon, juiced

2 teaspoons of minced fresh dill

A pinch of salt and crushed black pepper

Preparation:

Preheat an oven to a temperature of 350°F. Lightly grease a baking pan with oil and set aside.

Combine together all ingredients for the meatball until well combined and from into 2-inch balls. Transfer on the prepared baking pan and bake for 25 minutes or until the meatballs are lightly browned.

While roasting the meatballs, add all sauce ingredients in a food processor and pulse until smooth and well incorporated. Transfer to a bowl and set aside.

When the meatballs are done. Transfer into a serving platter and pour Tzatziki sauce to cover the meatballs.

Serve immediately.

Nutrition information per serving: Kcal: 441 Protein: 18.3g, Carbs: 7.1g, Fats: 38.2g

31. Coconut Chicken Satay

Ingredients:

1 pound of free range chicken breasts, sliced into strips

4 tablespoons of toasted shredded coconut

For the sauce

½ cup of tahini sauce

½ cup coconut milk

2 tablespoons of organic lime juice

½ tablespoon of minced garlic

1 jalapeno pepper, seeds removed and chopped

¼ teaspoon of chili powder

Preparation:

Preheat an oven to high with a broiler setup and position the rack on the top. Line a baking sheet with foil and set aside. Add all sauce ingredients in a food processor and pulse into a coarse mixture. Transfer to a bowl and set aside. Insert 4 to 5 chicken strips on each skewer, brush with ¼ sauce mixture evenly on all areas and place it on the prepared baking sheet.

Place the baking sheet with chicken on the rack and broil

for 5 minutes. Open the broiler and turn the skewers, brush with another ¼ cup sauce. Broil for 5 to 6 minutes more and remove from the oven when cooked through.

Transfer on a serving platter and pour with the remaining sauce on top. Sprinkle with toasted shredded coconut and serve warm.

Nutrition information per serving: Kcal: 261 Protein: 25.5g, Carbs: 10.2g, Fats: 14.1g

32. Baked Garlic Chicken with Mushrooms

Ingredients:

1 ½ pounds of skinless chicken thighs

½ pound of sliced cremini mushrooms

1 cup homemade chicken stock

1 medium head of garlic, crushed and peeled

2 tablespoons of clarified butter or ghee

½ teaspoon of onion powder

½ teaspoon of dried sage leaves

¼ teaspoon of cayenne pepper

¼ teaspoon of crushed black pepper

¼ teaspoon of salt

Preparation:

Preheat an oven to a temperature of 375°F. Season chicken with salt and pepper and stead aside.

In an ovenproof pan, apply high heat and add 1 tablespoon of ghee. Once the ghee is hot, sear both sides of the chicken for 2 minutes. Remove from the pan and transfer to plate and set aside.

Add the remaining ghee in the same pan and apply medium-high heat. Sauté the garlic until lightly brown and fragrant. Stir in the mushrooms, pour in the stock and cook until it reaches to a boil. Remove from pan, transfer to a plate and set aside. Return chicken into the pan and spread the mushrooms evenly over the chicken. Season with salt and pepper and bake it in the oven for 15 minutes, or until the chicken is cooked through. Remove the chicken and transfer to a serving platter. Transfer the mushrooms and all contents from the pan into a food processor and pulse until smooth and thick.

Pour the gravy on top of the chicken and serve immediately.

Nutrition information per serving: Kcal: 402 Protein: 51.4g, Carbs: 7.9g, Fats: 20.1g

33. Creamy Pumpkin Beef Soup

Ingredients:

1 tablespoon of ghee

1 pound of ground grass-fed beef

1 onion, halved crosswise and thinly sliced

2 jalapeno peppers, seeded and diced

2 large zucchini, cut into cubes

4 cups of homemade beef stock

2 ½ cups of tomato sauce

2 cups of pureed pumpkin

½ tablespoon of garlic powder

½ tablespoon of dried oregano

Preparation:

Add half of the ghee in a large pot and apply medium-high heat. Brown the beef for 6 to 7 minutes or until cooked through. Remove from the pot and transfer into a bowl. Add the remaining ghee into the pot and sauté the onions, peppers and zucchini for 5 minutes, or until the vegetables are soft and tender. Add a tablespoon of water, cook while scraping the browned bits on the bottom of the pan.

Return the beef, pour in the pureed pumpkin, tomato sauce and the stock and bring it to a boil. Reduce to low heat, season with salt, garlic powder and oregano and simmer for 15 to 20 minutes while stirring occasionally.

Once the soup has thickened, remove from heat and portion into individual serving bowls. Top with extra oregano and serve warm.

Nutrition information per serving: Kcal: 80 Protein: 4.3g, Carbs: 16g, Fats: 1.4g

34. Roasted Garlic & Artichoke Stuffed Chicken

Ingredients:

6 chicken breast fillets, butterfly cut

½ cup chopped baby spinach

For the stuffing

8 garlic cloves, crushed and peeled

10 medium artichokes

1 teaspoon of salt

½ teaspoon of ground white pepper

1 cup packed of minced fresh parsley

4 tablespoons of ghee or extra virgin olive oil

Preparation:

Preheat gas grill to high heat and brush the grid with oil. Add all ingredients for the stuffing except for the oil in a food processor and pulse into a coarse mixture. Pulse again and gradually add the oil until well incorporated.

Stuff each breast with equal amounts of artichoke mixture and chopped baby spinach.

Slowly fold the breast fillet back together and secure the edge with soaked wooden skewer. Season with salt and white pepper and drizzle with extra oil on top.

Reduce grill temperature to medium and grill the chicken for 6 minutes on each side while turning to cook the sides evenly. Turn to cook the raw side for another 5 minutes and check for doneness.

Once the chicken is done, transfer to serving platter and serve with extra chopped parsley on top.

Nutrition information per serving: Kcal: 514 Protein: 44.8g, Carbs: 14.8g, Fats: 32.1g

35. Pumpkin Custard

Ingredients:

1 ½ cups of coconut milk

½ cup of coarsely chopped almonds or pecans

2 ripe yellow bananas, sliced

3 tablespoons of almond butter

4 eggs

¼ teaspoon of cinnamon

1 ½ cups of pumpkin puree

Preparation:

Preheat the oven to 350°F.

Add all ingredients in a mixing bowl, blend with a hand mixer on medium speed for about 5 minutes or until well combined. Transfer on a greased baking dish and top with chopped nuts. Bake it in the oven for 30 minutes or until thoroughly cooked. Remove from the oven and let it stand for 10 minutes.

Chill for at least 30 minutes before serving or serve warm.

Nutrition information per serving: Kcal: 207 Protein: 87.9g, Carbs: 48g, Fats: 20g

36. White omelet

Ingredients:

1 teaspoon of olive oil

1 cup of egg whites, beaten (free range)

1 cup of shredded cooked chicken breast

1 ripe apple, cored and peeled, diced

½ cup shredded collard greens

2 tablespoons of toasted crushed hazelnuts

A pinch of salt and black pepper

Preparation:

In a pan, apply medium-high heat and add the oil. Add the chicken, season with salt and pepper and cook until the meat is golden brown. Stir in the apples and cook for 1 minute or until soft and tender. Transfer to a plate and set aside. Add the collard greens in the pan, cook for 1 minute and return the chicken and apple. Pour the egg whites in the skillet, swirl to spread evenly on the bottom of the pan and top with crushed hazelnuts. Cover and reduce to low heat. Cook for about 5 minutes or until the eggs are set and cooked through.

Slide it on a serving plate and serve the omelette

immediately.

Nutrition information per serving: Kcal: Protein: 4.4g, Carbs: 23g, Fats: 3g

37. Salmon with tomatoes

Ingredients:

1 cup cherry tomatoes, diced

1 tablespoon olive oil

4 salmon fillets (about 6 ounce each)

2 tablespoons red curry paste

¼ cup fresh basil, torn into pieces

A pinch of salt and black pepper

Preparation:

Preheat an oven to a temperature of 400°F. Lightly grease a rimmed baking sheet with oil and set aside. Add together the diced tomatoes, black pepper, salt and 1 tablespoon of red curry paste in a mixing bowl and then toss to combine. Place it on the greased baking sheet and spread it evenly.

Lightly coat the fillets with the remaining curry paste and sprinkle with salt and pepper on both sides. Place the fillets on top of the tomato mixture and roast it in the oven for about 20 minutes. It is done if the fish flakes easily when a fork is inserted and twisted on the meat.

Transfer the fish and tomatoes on a serving platter. Serve warm with chopped basil on top.

Nutrition information per serving: Kcal: 248 Protein: 34.7g, Carbs: 3.6g, Fats: 9.7g

38. Broccoli soup

Ingredients:

1 cup of chopped broccoli

1 small carrot

1 small onion

Salt

Pepper

Oil

Preparation:

Wash the onions and carrots, but do not chop them. Put them together with the broccoli in salted water and cook. When the vegetables are done, put them all together in a blender. Remaining vegetable water heat to boiling point and stir with a little oil. Cook until the mixture thickens, add the vegetables and cook for another 5-7 minutes. Serve warm.

Nutrition information per serving: Kcal: 150 Protein: 5.2g, Carbs: 15.4g, Fats: 7g

39. Coconut lamb

Ingredients:

½ cup Extra Virgin Coconut Oil (Hard Pressed)

1 green pepper, diced

1 yellow pepper, diced

A pinch of salt and pepper

1.5 pound of lamb chops

1 cup of green olives

6 tomatoes, sliced

1 onion, peeled

A dash of parsley

Preparation:

Heat the oil in a saucepan. To the oil, add peppers, tomatoes, salt, olives, pepper, parsley and onion.

Sauté the lamb chops in a separate pan. Once sautéed, transfer to the saucepan.

Adjust the spices and your coconut lamb is ready.

Nutrition information per serving: Kcal: 280 Protein: 15.9g, Carbs: 23.6g, Fats: 14g

40. Rice pasta with kale

Ingredients:

8 cups of Kale, cut finely with stems removed

2 grape tomatoes, halved

6 oz rice flour spaghetti

1/3 cup of chopped roasted almonds

2 tbsp of olive oil

2 chopped garlic cloves

¼ cup grated Pecorino

1 red onion, sliced

A pinch of black pepper and Himalayan crystal salt

Preparation:

Boil the spaghetti as per the instructions on the packet. Drain the spaghetti but retain ¼ cup of the water.

Take a large skillet and put over medium-high heat. Pour the olive oil. Once the oil is hot, add the salt, pepper, garlic and onion. Cook the ingredients till brown which should take around 5 minutes. Then throw in the kale and cook for a further 3 minutes or so till the kale is tender. Put the tomatoes in and cook till tomatoes are soft.

Top it off with Himalayan Crystal Salt to enhance its nutritional value for you.

Pour this mixture along with the spaghetti water over the pasta and put the other ingredients on top. Toss the spaghetti to mix the ingredients well.

Nutrition information per serving: Kcal: 314 Protein: 9.6g, Carbs: 38.8g, Fats: 14.6g

41. Wild Alaskan salmon fillet

2 pieces of wild Alaskan salmon fillets, around 3.5lbs each

1 tbsp of red pepper

1 tbsp of chili powder

2 tbsp Himalayan crystal salt

1 tbsp of ground nutmeg

1 tbsp of garlic powder

1 tbso of black pepper

1 ½ tbspof brown sugar

2 tbsp of celery seed

2 tbsp of dried marjoram

Preparation:

This recipe is incredibly easy to make as you will see in the steps below:

Rub all the spices over the fleshy side of the salmon. Be generous and make sure you cover the entire flesh with spices. Apply a coat of olive oil after the spices have been rubbed in properly.

Put the salmon on the grill. The side on which you applied the spices has to be down. Cook both sides of the salmon for around 10 minutes and tuck in!

Nutrition information per serving: Kcal: 131 Protein: 4.4g, Carbs: 23g, Fats: 3g

42. Blueberries beef burgers

Ingredients:

12 oz of ground beef

2 teaspoons of mustard

A pinch of himalayan crystal salt and pepper

1/3 cup of fresh blueberries

1 teaspoon of organic tomato sauce

2 minced garlic cloves

Burger buns

Preparation:

Put the blueberries along with the tomato sauce, salt, pepper, mustard, vinegar and garlic in your food processor and blend. Then pour the mixture out into a large bowl.

Add the beef into the bowl and mash it with the other ingredients. Divide the mixture into portions large enough to make patties for your burgers.

Put the patties on the grill and cook for 5 minutes on each side. Place the patties in the gluten-free buns and add any toppings you like.

Nutrition information per serving: Kcal: 206 Protein: 18.6g, Carbs: 13.7g, Fats: 9.1g

43. Mushroom steak

Ingredients:

1 ½ pounds of grass fed beef flank steaks

2 red bell peppers, chopped

1 white onion, halved crosswise and then thinly sliced

8 ounces of quartered mushrooms

2 teaspoons minced garlic

2 pinches of ground cumin

2 pinches of chili powder

1 ripe avocado, sliced

1 tablespoon of ghee

Salt and crushed black pepper

For the marinade

3 tablespoons of extra virgin olive oil

2 teaspoons of minced garlic

3 tablespoons of organic lime juice

½ teaspoon of ground cumin

½ teaspoon of chili powder

½ teaspoon of cayenne pepper

½ teaspoon salt

½ teaspoon crushed black pepper

Preparation:

Combine together all marinade ingredients in a bowl, add the steak and toss to coat evenly with the marinade mixture. Chill for at least 1 hour in the fridge.

Preheat gas grill to medium-high heat. Remove the steak from the marinade and grill for 5 to 6 minutes on each side. Turn and cook the other side for 5 minutes, transfer to a cutting board and let it rest.

In a pan, apply medium-high heat and add the ghee. Sauté the onions, garlic and bell pepper for 5 minutes and stir in the mushrooms. Cook for 2 minutes and stir in the cumin and chilli powder. Season with salt and pepper, cook for 2 minutes and remove from heat.

Thinly slice the steaks across the grain and place it on a serving platter. Add the sautéed vegetables and avocado and serve immediately.

Nutrition information per serving: Kcal: 265 Protein: 34.7g, Carbs: 9.7g, Fats: 9.1g

44. Lamb chops

Ingredients:

2 pounds of grass-fed lamb loin chops

Salt and crushed black pepper

For the Marinade

6 crushed garlic cloves

1 red onion, diced

1 tablespoon of minced fresh rosemary leaves

2 Scotch bonnet peppers, seeded and diced

1 medium scallion, chopped

1 teaspoon of allspice mix

2 tablespoons of extra virgin olive oil

Preparation:

Combine together all marinade ingredients in a food processor and pulse into a coarse mixture. Transfer into a bowl and set aside.

Season meat with salt and pepper on both sides and add it into the marinade. Coat evenly with the mixture and chill for at least an hour.

Preheat gas grill to medium-high heat and lightly brush the grid with oil. Grill the lamb chops for 8to 10 minutes on each side, turn and cook the other side for another 8 to 10 minutes. Check doneness and transfer to a plate.

Let it rest for5 minutes before serving.

Nutrition information per serving: Kcal: 226 Protein: 15.9g, Carbs: 2g, Fats: 17.6g

45. Grilled Pork Chops & Sweet Potatoes

Ingredients:

For the Sweet Potato

2 medium sweet potatoes, quartered

1 tablespoon of extra virgin olive oil

½ teaspoon of red pepper

½ teaspoon of ground cinnamon

A pinch of salt

A pinch of crushed black pepper

For the Pork Chop

4 organic pork chops

½ tablespoon of red pepper

Salt and crushed black pepper

For the Mango Sauce

½ cup pureed ripe mango

1 tablespoon of ghee

1 tablespoon of apple cider vinegar

A pinch of ground black pepper

Preparation:

Add all sauce ingredients in a saucepan and apply medium heat. Cook for 5 minutes or until it reaches to a boil while stirring occasionally. Transfer to a bowl and set aside.

In a separate bowl, add the potatoes and sprinkle with dry ingredients. Add the oil and gently toss to distribute the seasonings. Season pork chops with pepper, salt and pepper on both sides and set aside.

Preheat gas grill to medium-high heat and brush the grids with oil. Grill potatoes on one side of the grill and the pork chops on the other side. Take ½ of the mango sauce and brush both sides of the meat while grilling.

Grill the potatoes for 10 minutes on each side and turn to cook the other side for 10 minutes. Grill the pork chops for 6 to 8 minutes on each side, turn to cook the other side for another 6 minutes or until cooked through.

Place the pork chops and potatoes on a serving platter and serve with the reserved mango sauce.

Nutrition information per serving: Kcal: 470 Protein: 40.1 g, Carbs: 65.5g, Fats: 6g

46. Grilled T-Bones Steaks

Ingredients:

4 beef T-bone steaks

Extra virgin olive oil, for greasing

2 tablespoons of smoked paprika

1 teaspoon of onion powder

1 teaspoon of garlic powder

1 teaspoon of chili powder

1 teaspoon of ground coriander

½ teaspoon of salt

½ teaspoon of crushed black pepper

Preparation:

Preheat the gas grill to high heat and brush the grid with oil. Combine together all dry rub ingredients in a bowl. Rub the mixture evenly on both sides of the steak and grill for 5 to 6 minutes on each side. Turn to cook the other side for another 5 to 6 minutes and check internal temperature for the desired doneness. Transfer on a plate, cover with foil and let it rest for 10 minutes before serving.

Nutrition information per serving: Kcal: 171 Protein: 13g, Carbs: 18.3g, Fats: 5.2g

47. Lemon spiced grilled shrimps

Ingredients:

1 pound of fresh peeled and deveined shrimps

1 organic lemon, sliced into wedges for serving

1 tablespoon of minced fresh parsley, for serving

For the Marinade

4 tablespoons of ghee or extra virgin olive oil

1 teaspoon of minced garlic

2 tablespoons of organic lemon juice

½ teaspoon of salt

½ teaspoon of crushed black pepper

½ teaspoon of dried thyme leaves

½ teaspoon of dried oregano

Preparation:

Combine together all marinade ingredients in a medium bowl and mix until well combined. Place the shrimp and coat evenly with the marinade mixture. Cover the bowl and chill for at least 1 hour to marinate the shrimps.

Preheat gas grill to high heat and brush the grids with oil.

Insert 2 to 3 shrimps on each skewer, brush with marinade and grill for 3 minutes on each side. Turn to cook the other side for another 3 minutes and transfer into a serving platter.

Serve warm with lemons wedges and sprinkle with minced parsley.

Nutrition information per serving: Kcal: 112 Protein: 1.1g, Carbs: 2.7g, Fats: 11.6g

ADDITIONAL TITLES FROM THIS AUTHOR

70 Effective Meal Recipes to Prevent and Solve Being Overweight: Burn Fat Fast by Using Proper Dieting and Smart Nutrition

By

Joe Correa CSN

48 Acne Solving Meal Recipes: The Fast and Natural Path to Fixing Your Acne Problems in Less Than 10 Days!

By

Joe Correa CSN

41 Alzheimer's Preventing Meal Recipes: Reduce or Eliminate Your Alzheimer's Condition in 30 Days or Less!

By

Joe Correa CSN

70 Effective Breast Cancer Meal Recipes: Prevent and Fight Breast Cancer with Smart Nutrition and Powerful Foods

By

Joe Correa CSN

www.ingramcontent.com/pod-product-compliance
Lightning Source LLC
Chambersburg PA
CBHW052033070526
44584CB00016B/2021